Collins

Robbie Gibbons
and
Alan Gibbons

Chapter 1

Her red hair caught Danny's eye as he glanced out the window. He'd seen her before, waiting at the bus stop outside the shop. Tonight, she was late. The last bus running had already passed ten minutes ago. Maybe he should tell her.

The girl's eyes flicked towards him as she caught him looking; he quickly went back to wiping the tables. What was he thinking? He was trying to stay invisible. If anyone knew his true identity …

That's why he worked here, in Khan's Kebabs. His boss Samir didn't ask too many questions.

It was only a few minutes until his shift was over. It was getting dark. He was hungry. And not for the type of meat Samir sold in plastic trays. This was when Danny had to be most careful.

"It's closing time, Mark," Samir said.

Mark Smith. That was Danny's new name. Sounds normal, right? That's what he wanted. Normal. Dull. Invisible.

He flipped the sign on the door to "Closed". The girl outside was on her smartphone – probably texting her boyfriend. Girls like that always had boyfriends. She had full lips and a slightly crooked tooth. Imperfectly pretty. She looked almost good enough to …

Uh-oh.

Hunger pulled at Danny's stomach. Suddenly everything felt threatening: the heat inside the shop, the red of the plastic chairs, the heavy smell of sizzling meat that still hung in the air.

Danny tore off his apron and tossed it behind the counter. "See you tomorrow, Samir."

Without waiting for a reply, he burst out of the shop. He ran past the girl without looking. He didn't stop until he escaped the streetlights and was swallowed by the night.

Chapter 2

As he ran, memories clawed at him. Memories of his past life leapt out like small fires in the dark.

Danny stopped when he was a little way up into the surrounding hills. It wasn't too far from where he had made his camp, away from the prying eyes of the town.

In the cover of darkness, he felt calmer. His hunger eased a little. Looking back, he could still see the girl at the bus stop, standing in the fizzing light of the neon sign above Khan's. Waiting for a bus that wouldn't come.

A normal teenage boy would have gone over, chatted to her maybe. Telling her the last bus had already gone would've been a good excuse to get to know her.

Danny had barely spoken to anyone since he was forced to leave his hometown two months before. His chest tightened with a pang of regret. He missed his friends. He missed his mum. But he couldn't return.

Because Danny wasn't a normal teenage boy. Danny had a secret.

Chapter 3

The girl was walking off now. A few snowflakes danced in the frosty air. She took the country lane that wove through fields to the other side of town. Danny breathed a sigh as he watched her tread a lonely path through the dark.

He was about to move on – he longed for the earthy smell of the woods, the thrill of the hunt – but just before the girl dropped out of sight, he saw the dark shape following her. An animal.

There was something about the way the moonlight gleamed over the animal's fur, something about the rise and fall of the hunched shoulders.

Danny strained his eyes against the dark, but the girl and her stalker had disappeared under the branches of arched trees. He found himself edging back down the slope. He peered at the dark form. It couldn't be. Not here.

His pulse quickened. He ran towards her. As he did so, a warm rush surged through his body. The shift had begun. His skin burst with pain as hairs sprouted all over. Teeth and claws ripped free. Before he knew it, he was crashing through the grass on four legs.

This was Danny's secret.

Chapter 4

Danny followed his senses, tearing through grass and brambles. A scream pierced the air. He found them in a ditch by the side of the road. The girl was pinned, helpless. The animal on top of her was too big to be an ordinary wolf: razor claws, a muscular, human-like upper body. It was a werewolf, like Danny. His nightmare had followed him here, to a place where he thought he was safe.

Just beyond them, cars zoomed past with no idea of the scene unfolding in the dark of the roadside.

Danny's momentum carried him towards them. He moved by instinct. He ran faster than he could think. Sensing his approach, the attacker raised its ghastly head. Their eyes met and Danny saw something that could have been recognition in the beast's stare.

A split second later, he crashed headfirst into the wolf and sent it sprawling into the road. It rolled onto its back, legs kicking in panic.

Then, the blare of a horn. The screech of brakes. A flash of white as headlights cut through the darkness. The lorry smashed into the attacker with a sickening crunch. The twisting form trembled. The head fell back.

As the vehicle rumbled to a stop, Danny's breath caught in his throat. The body left broken on the tarmac was no longer a wolf. It was human. The face was one he recognised. It was one of Jay Carver's old gang.

The shock of seeing somebody he knew knocked the fight out of Danny. The wolf in him retreated. His fur shrank back.

The girl was still lying in the grass, horrified and frozen. Their eyes locked for a moment. Danny heard the slam of the lorry door. Somebody was coming. If he didn't leave now, the driver would see him.

"Please, tell no one," he said.

Chapter 5

Back at his camp, Danny looked through his backpack. He was down to his last pair of jeans. His clothes from last night had been shredded to useless rags during the shift. It was one of the downsides to being a werewolf.

His camp was in the ruins of an old priory in the hills above the town. This was where he had thought he could hide from the world.

The building was little more than a shell. Parts of the walls had crumbled away and some of the ceilings had already fallen. The whole thing was chained off, with signs saying "Danger. Keep out." Danny hoped they would be enough to scare people off.

Danny needed to go into town. He was out of toothpaste, too. Waking up with the taste of raw meat in your mouth was another downside to being a werewolf. But he couldn't risk going into town any time soon. The night's events had got in the way of his hunting pattern. He was hungry. And when he was hungry, he was a danger to everyone.

The wage from his job in Khan's was enough for the few supplies he needed – clothes, toothpaste, soap. Apart from that, Danny didn't need money to survive. He kept his wolfish appetites at bay by hunting squirrels and rabbits in the forest. He slept in the hills in wolf-form. His fur was enough to keep him warm. But he was more than just an animal. At least, that's what he told himself.

That's why Danny still spent his daylight hours in the town. He had to remind himself he had a human side. If the animal ever had full control, he would be nothing but a cold-blooded killer. He would be like Carver.

Danny perched on one of the stones. He couldn't stop thinking about what had happened the night before. He remembered Carver, the psycho from his hometown who had turned out to be more than just a bully. Carver was the werewolf who had attacked Danny, who had turned Danny into what he was.

The wolf that got hit by the lorry was one of Carver's gang. They called him Bomber. Danny pictured the rest of the gang's faces and tried to match them with names. There was Lukas, who was always by Carver's side, and two more whose names Danny didn't know.

He remembered how the five of them were never apart. Carver's voice echoed in his mind: *Did you think I was the only one?* Of course, they were all werewolves. Danny had been stupid to think Carver was the only one. After all, didn't wolves hunt in packs? But why was one of them here, of all places?

As soon as he thought it, the answer sank to the pit of his stomach. They were looking for him. And if one of them had got this far, they were close.

Chapter 6

Danny couldn't sleep. Faces haunted him. He saw Carver and Lukas in his thoughts. He saw Bomber and the girl. He saw Mum.

The wolf he had inside scared him. The wolf had blood on its paws. He had blood on his hands. He paced back and forth, reliving what had happened.

What had the driver seen? What if the police were already looking for him? Had the girl kept quiet as he had begged? He thought he had seen something in her eyes that he could trust, but how could he be sure?

He couldn't just sit there, waiting for them to come for him. He made his way down the slope, hiding in the shadows every time he heard a noise. He hurried through the bushes and looked along the road.

There were police vans with flashing blue lights. Officers were searching for clues. He watched them, then climbed to higher ground.

Danny tried to push the memories away, but it was all too familiar. A person dead. Flashing police lights, torches shining in the dark. This was what had happened in his hometown. This was why he had been forced to leave.

Would he have to leave again? He liked it here. He was just starting to piece his new life together. But if one member of Carver's pack had found him, the others couldn't be far behind. Could he really stay and face them?

He breathed the night air and remembered everything that had happened to him. It felt as if yellow wolf eyes were piercing the gloom. He heard padding paws in the wind. He felt sharp, cold claws in the night air. His hunters were coming.

At that moment, the beam of a torch swung towards him. He heard a voice. It was one of the police officers.

"Did you see something?" she asked.

A second officer arrived. He gazed up the slope, directing his own torch towards the spot where Danny was crouching.

"I thought I saw movement."

"Where?"

"Over to the left."

Danny's heart kicked. This was a bad idea. He should've stayed where he was. The priory was so far from the road, the police might not go that far. The torches continued to sweep up the slope.

Danny flattened himself on the ground and wriggled back the way he had come. The torches roamed the hillside. He pressed himself down, trying to force himself inside the earth. *Please. Don't let them see me.* Still the bright beams criss-crossed around him.

"Anything?" the woman PC asked.

The male officer shook his head. "You're seeing things."

Danny breathed a sigh of relief.

But in his mind, he could see the pack. The hunters were coming his way. They weren't like those police officers. They would never give up until they found him.

Chapter 7

The attack was front-page news. Danny grabbed a copy of the local paper that had been left on a park bench.

There was a photo of the girl – her name was Chloe Cooper – and the lorry driver. The report described a mystery rescuer who had saved a local young woman from a savage assault. To Danny's relief, there was no mention of wolves. There was, however, a detailed description of the rescuer. Thanks, Chloe, he thought.

How was he supposed to stay under the radar with stories like this all over the papers? He couldn't stick around. He would have to lie low for a while and plan his next move.

On his way back to camp, he decided to risk a stop at Khan's. Samir had given Danny a job when he needed one and he didn't ask questions about his past. Danny owed it to him to at least let him know that he wouldn't be coming in to work for a few days.

Outside Khan's, Danny froze. Through the window, he could see a red-haired girl sitting at one of the tables. It was Chloe.

She noticed him staring before he could move off. He quickened his pace.

"Wait," he heard her shout after him from the door. "Please, I need to talk to you."

Danny's chest tightened. What if he heard Chloe out? What if he let another person into his life?

It wasn't an option. She was a human. The wolf in him would always see her as nothing more than a piece of meat. As dinner.

He was a risk to her. And, as she knew his secret now, she was a risk to him.

He was a lone wolf for a reason.

He picked up speed. For the second time in a couple of days he found himself running away from this girl he barely knew.

Danny formed his plan: he would hunt, then gather his few belongings, rest, and set off for somewhere new first thing in the morning.
He wondered if this was going to be his whole life – always running away.

Chapter 8

Midnight. Danny was woken by a distant voice calling his name. He was pretty sure it was Chloe. This girl was persistent. But there was a croak to her voice that put Danny on guard. She sounded frightened. Then came a second, male voice.

"Danny. We know you're out here somewhere."

In the distance, Danny could see Chloe. She was with three young men. Black shapes against the falling snow. A search party?

As they came closer he knew something was wrong. Chloe wasn't walking naturally; she was staggering. One of the lads had a grip of her hair, leading her up towards the trees. Like when Carver had led Danny into the forest on the night he had planned to kill him.

One of them pointed towards the priory. They headed in his direction. They were close enough for Danny to recognise them now, but he had already guessed. It was always going to come to this. It was Lukas and the remaining members of the gang.

Carver's wolf pack.

Danny had already put what little he had into a backpack. If he ran now, he could escape.

No. He couldn't leave Chloe. What if he ran and they took it out on her? He had to stay. For her sake. Besides, there was a reason he hadn't made his escape sooner. At the back of his mind he knew that if the pack had found him here, they could find him in the next place. Isn't that what wolves do? Hunt?

Danny was tired of running.

"I'm here," he shouted, but the quiver in his voice gave away his fear.

Chapter 9

"Let her go and I'll do whatever you want," Danny said, stepping out from the cover of the ruins.

"I told you bringing the girl would work," one of them muttered.

"Didn't your mum ever tell you not to play with your food?" jeered the other.

Lukas remained silent, breathing hatred.

"How did you find me?" Danny asked.

"We split up to hunt you down," one of them said. "Every town for miles. We hadn't heard from Bomber for a couple of days. Last time he phoned, he was here, so we came looking."

He unfolded a newspaper – yesterday's issue, with the report of the boy's death and Danny's description. "It was easy to put two and two together. You didn't make yourself hard to find."

"I'll do whatever you want," Danny repeated.

"We want you to die," Lukas said. "Blood for blood. You murdered Jay our brother. Bomber, too."

"You're the ones killing people," Danny shot back.

"What, *this*?" Lukas twisted his grip on Chloe's hair, making her wince in pain. "This is *food*, you idiot. You've climbed a step of the food chain and you don't even know it. You still think you're human." His voice rumbled into a growl. "You were supposed to be a meal. And now because of you, Jay and Bomber are dead."

Either side of him, the two began to shift. Their teeth sharpened into gruesome fangs. Their slim bodies exploded outwards, tearing their clothes into rags that fluttered away in the wind.

Danny underwent the same sudden, monstrous change. His bones snapped, his shoulders widened, his limbs stretched, his hands and teeth shaped into weapons.

Only Lukas remained in human form. He kept hold of Chloe and barked orders to the other two. "He's caused us too much trouble already. Make it quick."

Chapter 10

A chorus of howls broke the still night air. The two attackers split in a wide arc, coming at Danny from either side. He snapped his head back and forth, but couldn't keep them both in his sights.

Danny made a split-second decision. What did he have to lose? He burst to the left and charged the closest wolf. Defence turned into attack. They didn't expect that. He clashed with the wolf: ripping, clawing, biting.

The second wolf would be approaching fast. Danny managed to fix his jaws on his victim's neck. He clamped down just as the second wolf arrived and raked its claws deep across Danny's exposed ribs. Blood drops fell in the snow and bloomed like roses.

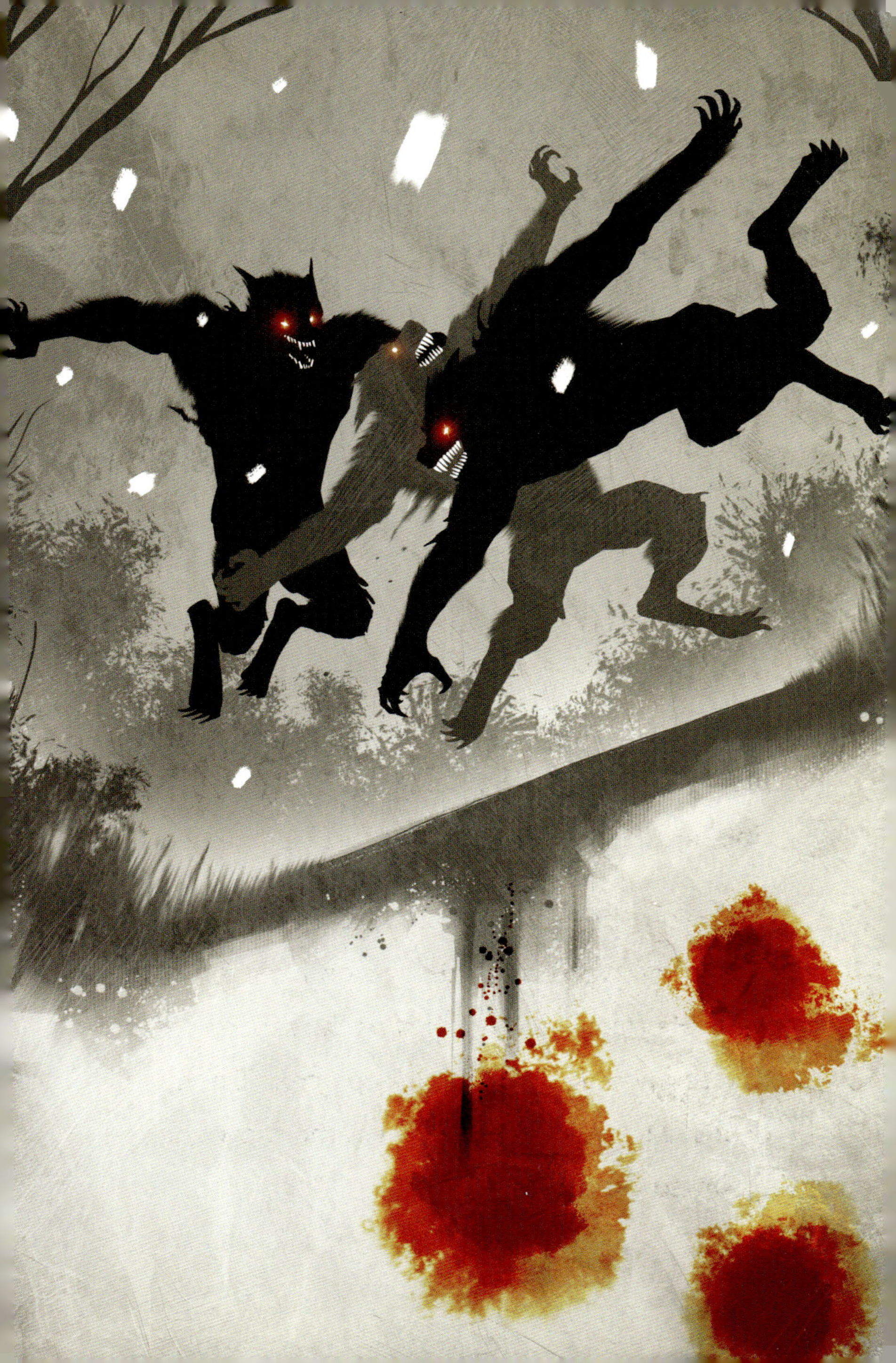

Danny shook himself free. The wolf he had bitten staggered a few yards, then dropped.
A blink later the animal was replaced by the body of a teenage boy, staining the snow with a pool of blood.

One down.

He turned his attention to the second hunter. Where was he?

Then there was a blur to his right.

The second wolf bounded towards him. Danny could feel the trickle of coppery blood on his fur. His strength was bleeding out of him. He wouldn't win in a fight. Instead, he retreated back to the cover of the priory. As he leapt over the chain barrier – "Danger. Keep out." – he had an idea.

The wolf chased him through the maze of stone. He leapt walls. He was fast. He was strong.

Danny led his enemy towards a part where he knew the wall was very unsafe. He waited for his moment.

One.

Two.

Three.

Danny heaved his bulk against the wall with all the strength he had left. The ceiling came crashing down on the following beast. A yelp of shock was cut dead as the falling rubble buried him.

Two down.

Chapter 11

With each heartbeat, Danny's lifeblood pumped out of him. The wound was deeper than he had first thought. The world was spinning. His strength was fading. He could hardly stand upright as he limped out into the snow to face his final opponent.

Lukas let out a howl of grief. He tossed Chloe aside as if she was weightless. He was already shifting from boy to demon. His face stretched into a monstrous snout. His bones cracked as his body twisted into its new form.

Lukas was the most terrifying werewolf Danny had seen. Ragged tufts of jet black hair. Yellow, bloodshot eyes that almost popped out of their skull.

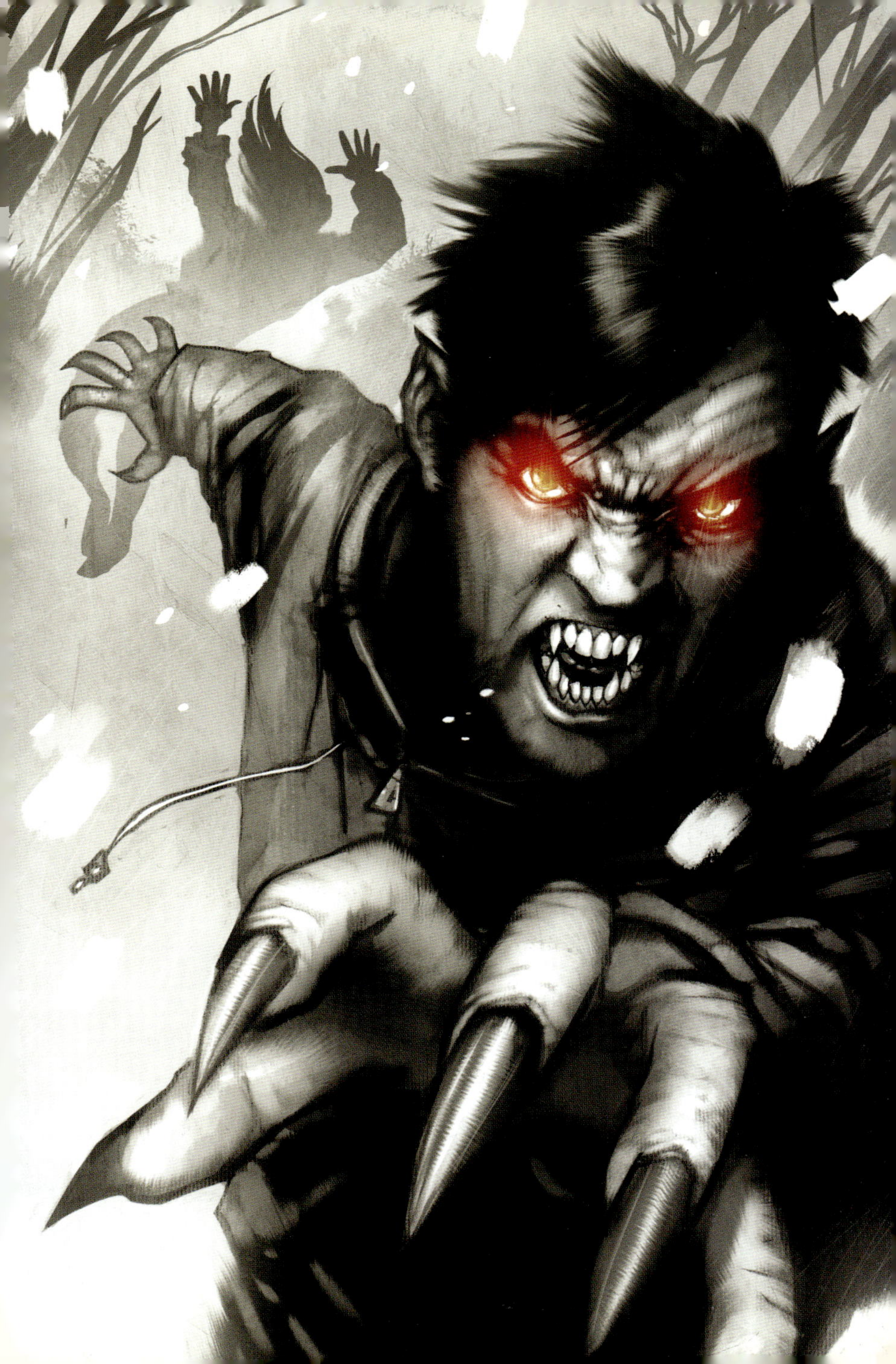

Danny knew he was beaten. He could see murder in the monster's eyes. Lukas had watched his pack fall one by one. Now he was a lone wolf, like Danny. Danny knew the power someone could find when they had nothing to lose.

Lukas exploded into a sprint. Danny could barely lift his paws to defend himself, and the charge sent him sprawling in the snow. His warm blood cooled on the cold, white ground. There was no fight left in him. His wolf self left him with a whimper.

Danny lay bleeding and half frozen in the snow. He was defenceless. Lukas snarled. Saliva dripped from his moon-white fangs. It was over.

Danny closed his eyes. He could feel the fangs against his neck, then a hot splash of blood. Then, nothing. No white light. Was this what death felt like?

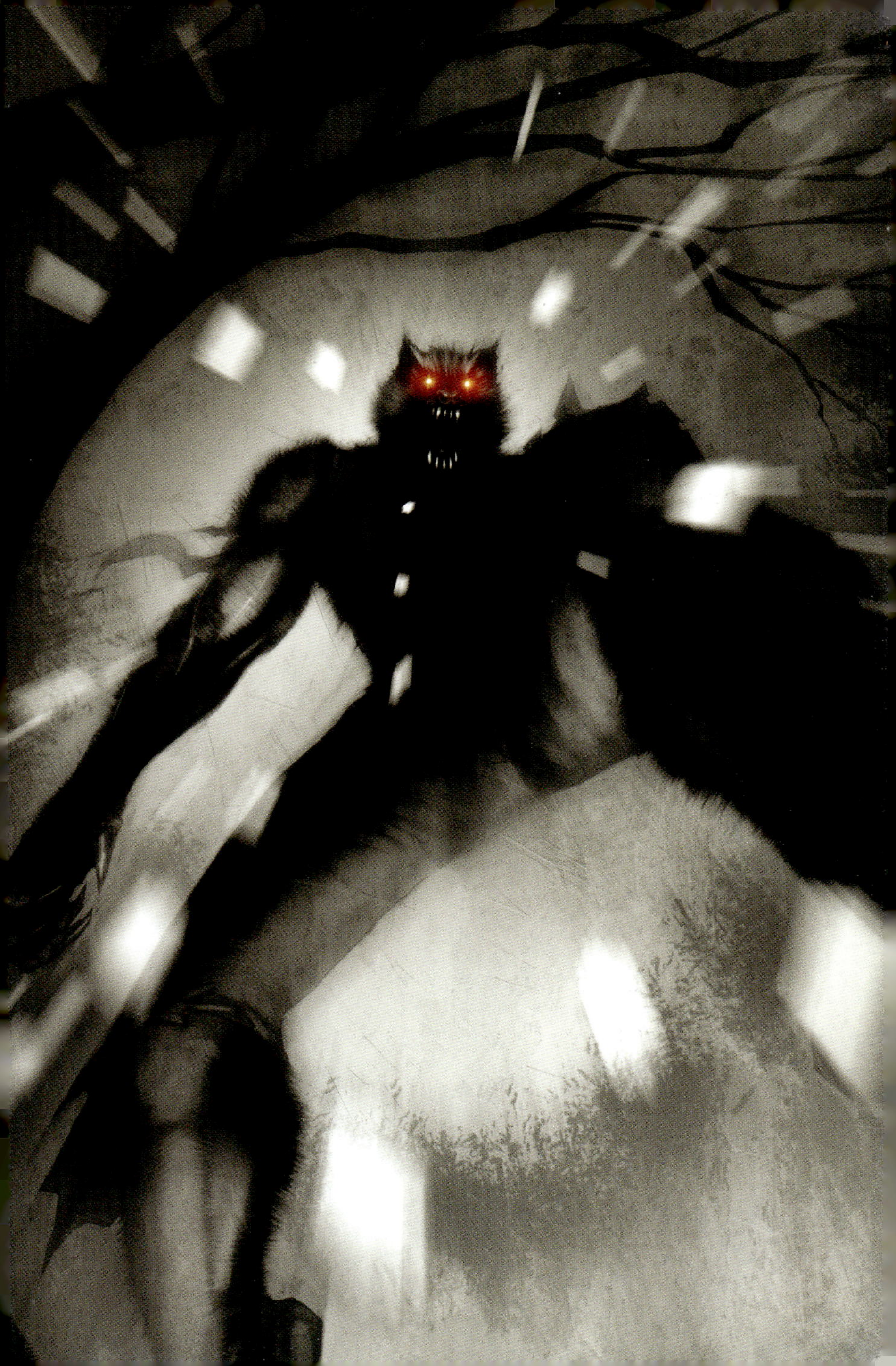

Danny opened his eyes. The blood wasn't his. Lukas was lying limp beside him. No longer a wolf, but a boy. His eyes were fixed into a lifeless stare. But how?

Danny's vision blurred. A face swam into focus. Another wolf! One with a sleek, fox-red coat. The strange wolf's features transformed, softened, until Danny found himself staring up at a familiar face.

"Chloe?"

Before he had a chance to think it through, Danny was overcome by a wave of exhaustion. The screech of the wind died as the world slipped away from him.

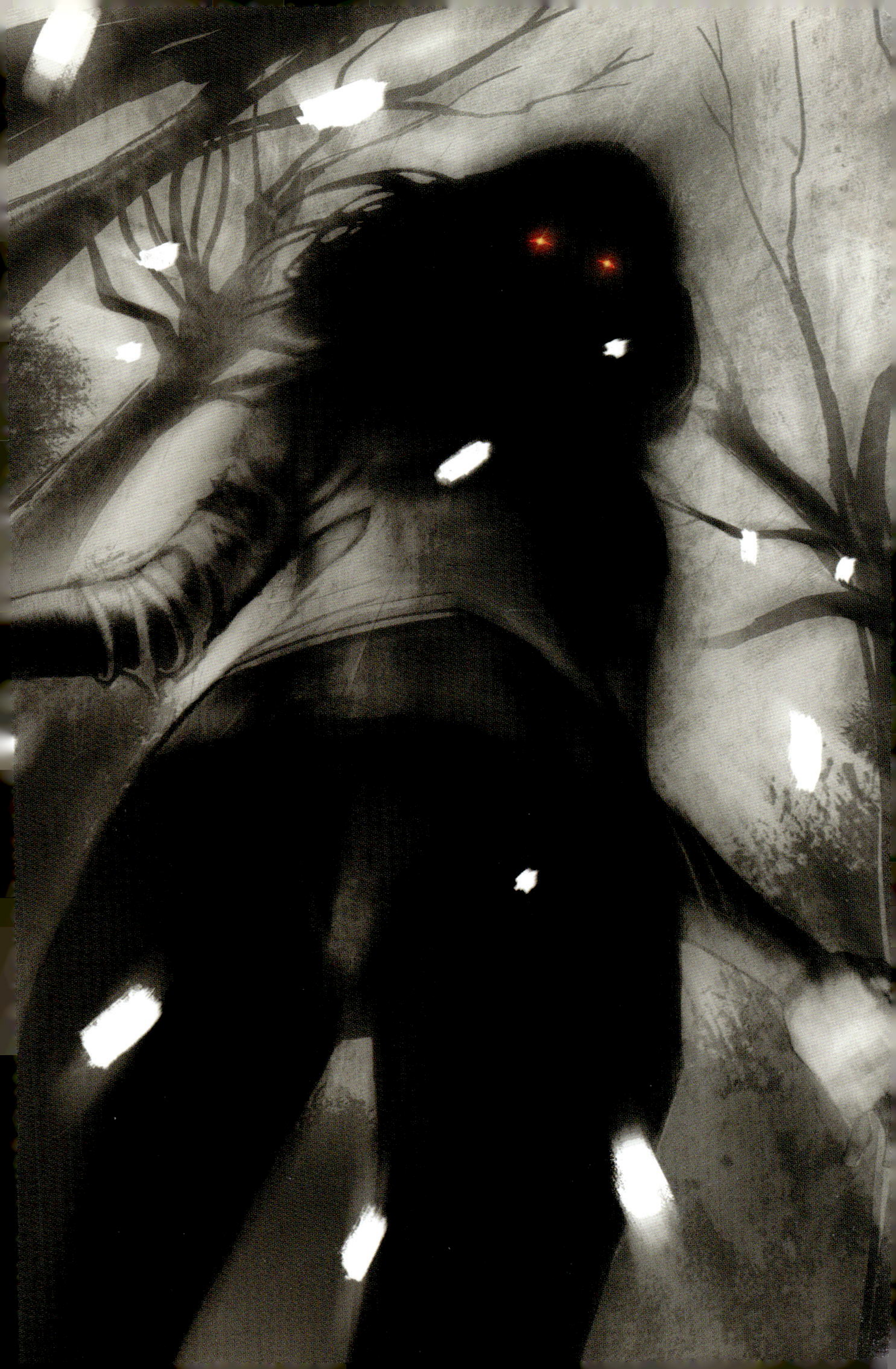

Chapter 12

When Danny woke, it was daylight. His head pounded. The chirp of birds was like needles in his ears. Chloe was gazing down at him.

"You stayed?"

"It was the least I could do."

Suddenly Chloe twisted round and stared into the distance. In the dawn light figures were approaching.

"More wolves?" Chloe asked.

Danny shook his head. "I don't think so."

There was the crackle of radios. Boots stamped down on the snowy ground. Sticks swished through the undergrowth.

"It's the police. Somebody must have heard the sounds of the struggle. Or maybe they're still searching the hills from the night I was attacked," Chloe said.

Danny felt the grip of panic. He pulled himself to his feet and stumbled away across the hill. The ground seemed to tilt and rock. He lurched against a tree trunk. He was swaying, hardly able to stand when a helping hand supported him. It was Chloe.

"You need to rest," she said. Danny looked down at his ribs, where the wolf's claws had torn into his flesh. The wounds were closing up.

"I can't stand here talking," Danny panted. "The police. They're coming this way."

He set off again. Once more, Chloe followed him. This time she put her arm round him and helped him to stagger a few hundred metres. "It's okay, they're still a long way from us."

"Why are you doing this?" Danny asked.

"Surely you know by now," Chloe said. She examined his wounds. "You're healing fast. Like, unnaturally fast. Is that one of our ..." she searched for the right word ... "powers?"

"*Our* powers," Danny repeated, frowning. The memories came flooding back. How Lukas was about to finish him off, when another wolf appeared from nowhere. It had been Chloe. She was a werewolf, like him.

Danny's head throbbed. A hundred questions buzzed in his head, but all he could manage to say was, "How?"

Chloe rolled up her sleeve to reveal the jagged scar on her arm. "It's from the first night we met, when I was attacked by the wolf."

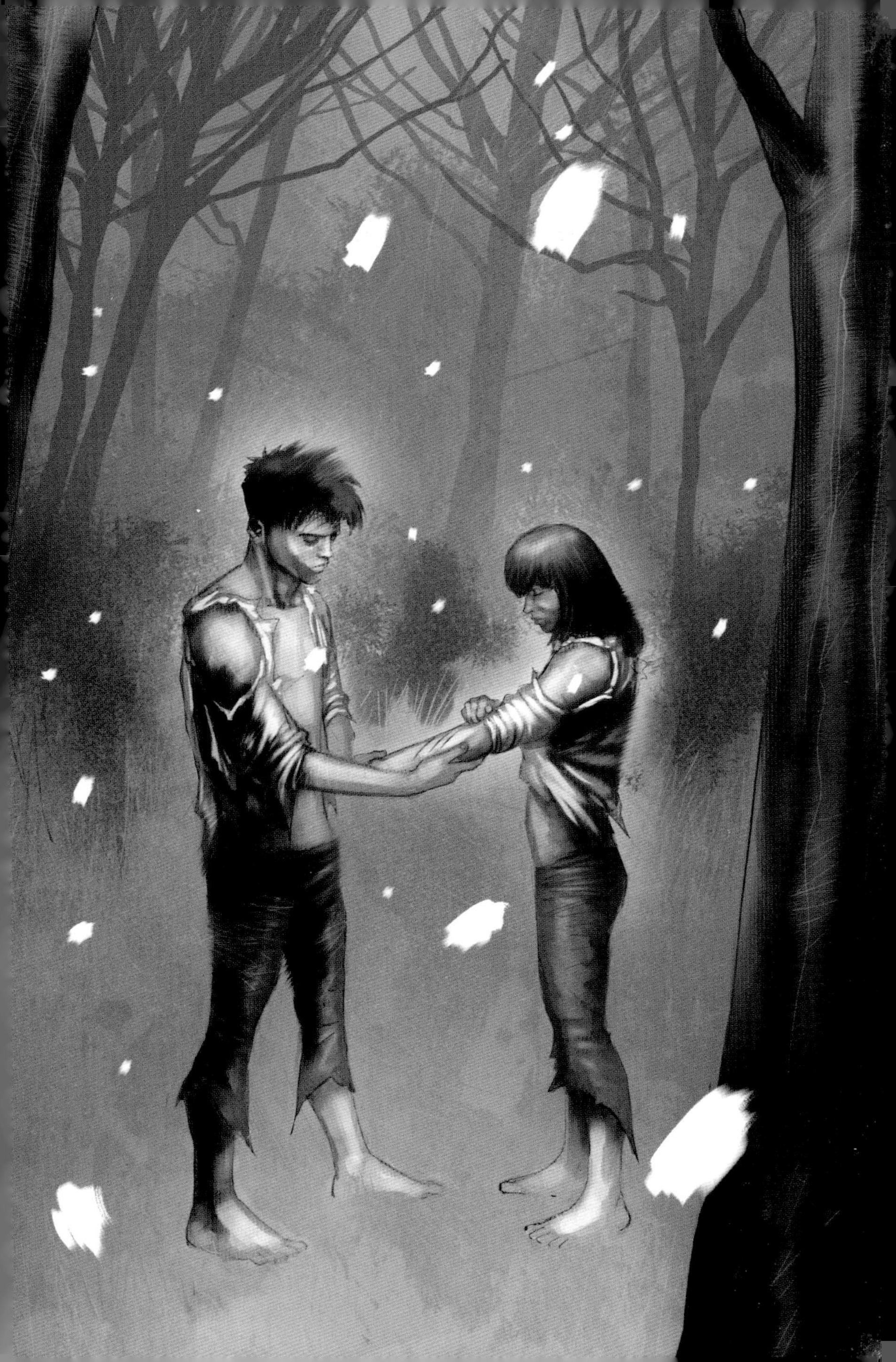

She told Danny how at first she had tried to deny it. Wolves turning into boys? It seemed crazy. But after the attack, she had started to feel different. She found herself drooling at the butcher's window, even though she was a vegetarian.

Chloe had gone looking for Danny, hoping he could give her an explanation. After he avoided her, she was kidnapped by Carver's pack.

Danny nodded. It all made sense.

Chloe said, "When the black wolf threw me onto the ground and attacked you, I knew it was over. He was going to kill you, and then he would kill me. That's when it happened."

"The shift," Danny said.

"Does it always hurt that much?"

"You get used to it," Danny told her.

"I guess there's a lot of things I'll have to get used to." Chloe looked out over the fields stretching to the horizon. "So where will we go?"

"We?"

"My old life is over. I know that. Who else have I got? I need you to help me."

Danny shook his head. She was serious. And it could actually work. As a pair, they could lose the police. As a pair, they could survive. He realised he would never have a normal life. He would always be running from the past. At least this way, he wouldn't be running alone.

"Okay," he said.

"I guess this makes us a pack?" said Chloe.

Danny laughed. The noise sounded strange to him. He realised it was the first time he'd laughed since he left home. And he knew why.

Because he was no longer a lone wolf.

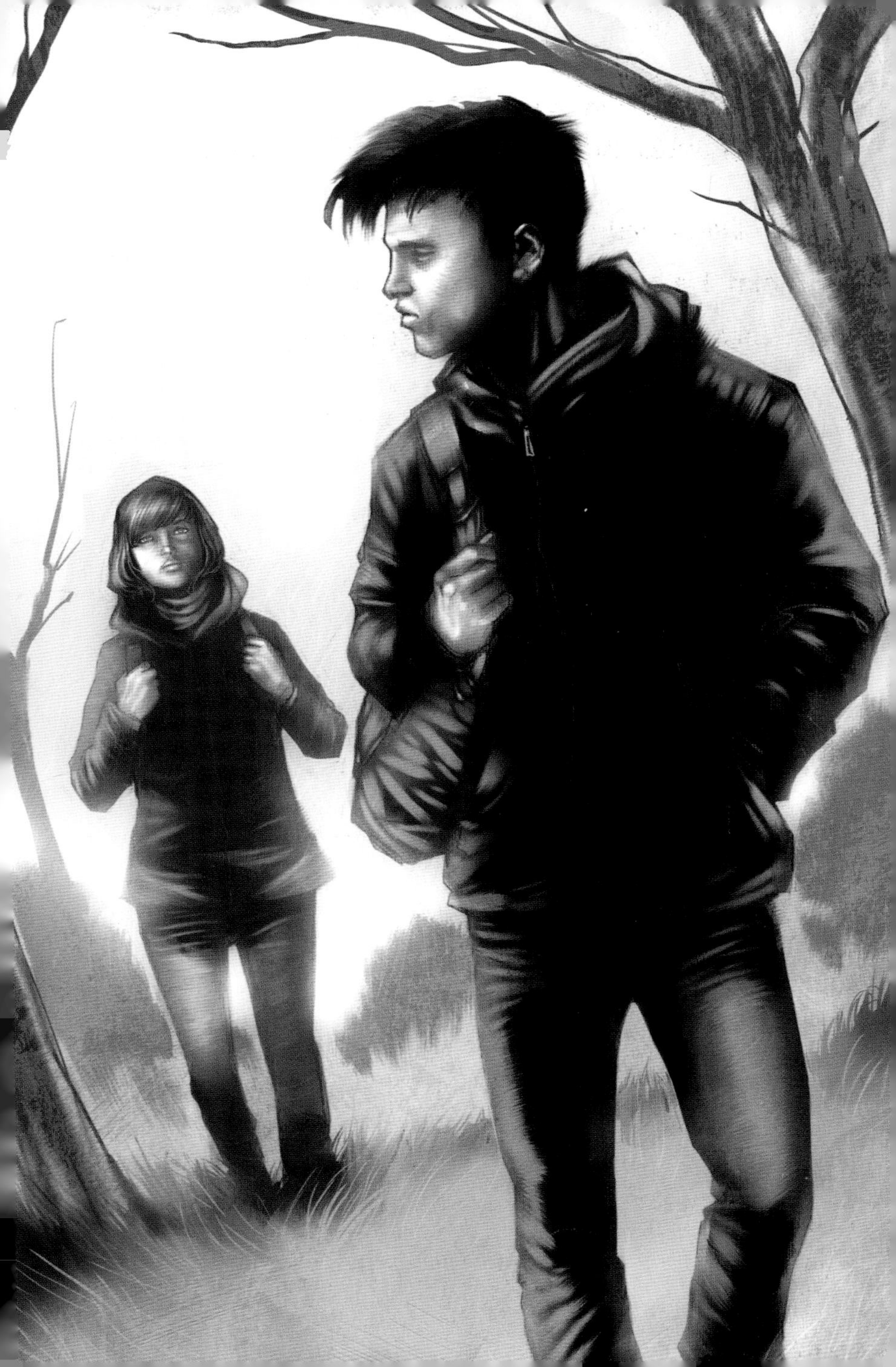

Reader challenge

Word hunt

1. On page 6, find an adjective that means "nosy" or "interfering".

2. On page 31, find a verb that means "laughed in a nasty way".

3. On page 40, find a verb that tells us Danny had difficulty walking.

Story sense

4. Why had Danny chosen to work in Khan's kebab shop? (page 3)

5. What things happened to Danny's body when the "shift" into a werewolf started? (page 10)

6. How do you think Danny felt when he saw the attack was front-page news? (page 24)

7. Why did Danny decide to stay and face the pack of wolves rather than run away? (page 30)

8. How do you think Danny felt when he realised Chloe had also become a wolf? Give reasons.

Your views

9. At what point in the story did you realise Chloe had also become a werewolf?

10. If you were the author of *On the Run*, would you have ended the story in the same way? Give reasons.

Spell it

With a partner, look at these words and then cover them up.

- breathed
- retreated
- heaved

Take it in turns for one of you to read the words aloud. The other person has to try and spell each word. Check your answers, then swap over.

Try it

With a partner, imagine one of you is Danny and the other is Chloe. Discuss what you will do next. Where will you go? How will you live? How will you keep out of danger?

William Collins's dream of knowledge for all began with the publication of his first book in 1819. A self-educated mill worker, he not only enriched millions of lives, but also founded a flourishing publishing house. Today, staying true to this spirit, Collins books are packed with inspiration, innovation and practical expertise. They place you at the centre of a world of possibility and give you exactly what you need to explore it.

Collins. Freedom to teach.

Published by Collins Education
An imprint of HarperCollins Publishers
77–85 Fulham Palace Road
Hammersmith
London
W6 8JB

Browse the complete Collins Education catalogue at **www.collins.co.uk**

Text by Alan Gibbons and Robbie Gibbons © HarperCollins *Publishers* 2014
Illustrations by Matt Timson © HarperCollins*Publishers* 2014

Series consultants: Alan Gibbons and Natalie Packer

10 9 8 7 6 5 4 3 2 1
ISBN 978-0-00-754618-3

All rights reserved. No part of this publication may be reproduced, stored in a retrieval system, or transmitted in any form or by any means, electronic, mechanical, photocopying, recording or otherwise, without the prior written permission of the Publisher or a licence permitting restricted copying in the United Kingdom issued by the Copyright Licensing Agency Ltd, 90 Tottenham Court Road, London W1T 4LP.

British Library Cataloguing in Publication Data.
A catalogue record for this publication is available from the British Library.

Commissioned by Catherine Martin
Edited by Sue Chapple
Project-managed by Lucy Hobbs and Caroline Green
Illustration management by Tim Satterthwaite
Proofread by Hugh Hillyard-Parker
Typeset by Jouve India, Ltd
Production by Emma Roberts
Printed and bound in China by South China Printing Co.
Cover design by Paul Manning

Acknowledgements

The publishers would like to thank the students and teachers of the following schools for their help in trialling the *Read On* series:
Park View Academy, London
Queensbury School, Queensbury, Bradford
Southfields Academy, London
St Mary's College, Hull
Ormiston Six Villages Academy, Chichester